BOMBS on BELFAST
THE BLITZ 1941

BOMBS on BELFAST

THE BLITZ 1941

In association with

Belfast **Telegraph**

NORTHERN IRELAND'S DAILY NEWSPAPER

Foreword by **Dr Ian Adamson OBE**

First published 1984 by
Pretani Press

This edition published 2011 by
Colourpoint Books

Colourpoint House, Jubilee Business Park
Jubilee Road, Newtownards, BT23 4YH
Tel: 028 9182 6339
Fax: 028 9182 1900
E-mail: info@colourpoint.co.uk
Web: www.colourpoint.co.uk

First Impression

Designed by April Sky Design, Newtownards
Tel: 028 9182 7195
Web: www.aprilsky.co.uk

Printed by GPS Colour Graphics, Belfast

ISBN 978-1-906578-91-6

Front cover: Bomb damage on High Street.

Explore, discover and buy other titles on Northern Ireland
subjects at BooksNI.com – the online bookshop for Northern Ireland

CONTENTS

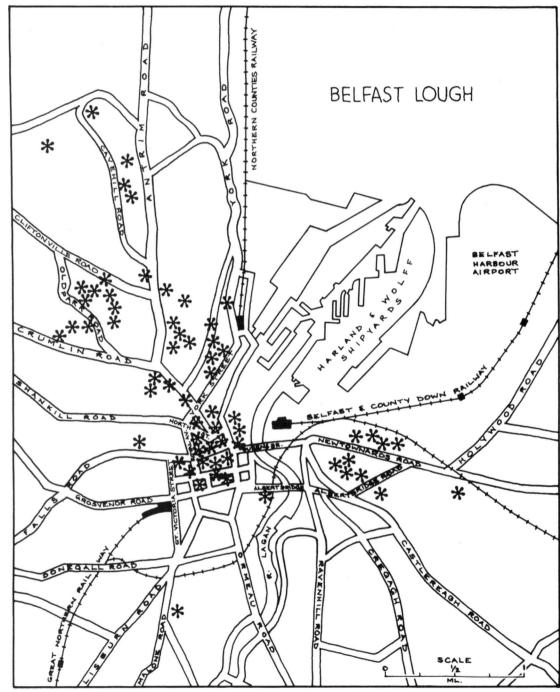

MAP OF BELFAST IN 1941

This map shows the locations of the photographs
contained in the book and indicates the main
civilian areas affected by the blitz.

FOREWORD

ON THE NIGHT of Easter Tuesday, 15th April 1941, as the result of its loyalty to Britain and her Empire, Belfast suffered the greatest single tragedy in its history – 160 bombers of the German Air Force (Luftwaffe) attacked the city. Some 900 people died and many were injured. In terms of damage to property, half the housing stock was affected and thousands were left homeless. It was the greatest loss of life, outside the City of London, in a night raid during the blitzing of the United Kingdom, and all sections of the community were affected.

Belfast was a prime target for the Nazis. Harland and Wolff was one of the largest shipbuilding yards in the world and had constructed many ships for the Royal Navy, including the aircraft carriers HMS *Formidable* and HMS *Unicorn*; the cruisers, HMS *Belfast* and the HMS *Penelope*, as well as 131 other naval vessels. About 35,000 people were employed. During the war Belfast yards built or converted at least 3,000 naval vessels, repaired more than 22,000 and launched 140 merchant ships, over half a million tons. Harland's also designed and built the Churchill tank. At the same time Short Brothers made the Short Sunderland flying boat and the Short Stirling long-range heavy bomber. They had been re-equipping as early as 1936 for the manufacture of 189 Handley Page Hereford bombers, and 20,000 people were employed.

James Mackie and Sons had been re-equipped in 1938 with new American machinery and became the prime supplier of Bofors ant-aircraft shells. Aero-linen for covering aircraft, such as the Hawker Hurricane and military glider frames, was manufactured by several Belfast flax spinning mills, such as The York Street Flax Spinning Co.; William Ewart's Rosebank Weaving Co.; Brookfield Spinning Co.; and the Linen Thread Co. The Sirocco Works at the Bridge End produced heating and ventilation equipment for the underground munition factories in Britain. Other factories manufactured gun mountings, ordnance pieces, aircraft parts and ammunition.

Belfast was ill prepared for the Blitz, with insufficient AA guns, few searchlights, inadequate air raid shelters, and far too few firemen, air raid wardens and civil defence members. It was like the *Titanic* disaster on the same day in 1912 all over again. The Government of Northern Ireland had neither the will or capacity to tackle such a major catastrophe. That Easter Tuesday few spectators would have noticed a lone Luftwaffe Junkers Ju-88b aircraft circling Windsor Park while Distillery F.C. were defeating Linfield F.C. by 3 goals to 1. The air-raid sirens first sounded at 10:40 pm. Wave after wave of German bombers dropped tons of high explosive bombs, parachute mines and incendiaries on the well nigh defenceless city. By 4:00 am the entire north of the city seemed to be in flames. At 4:45 am a telegram was sent asking the Irish Premier, de Valera for assistance. Although Eire was neutral, de Valera responded quickly. In all, 13 fire brigades were sent from Dublin, Dun Laoghaire, Dundalk and Drogheda. As well as Belfast, casualties were sustained in Londonderry, Bangor and Newtownards.

At 11:45 pm on the night of 4th May, the air-raid sirens sounded again. But on this occasion, by the time the first bombs fell at 1:02 am, most people apart from the essential services were sheltering. The Luftwaffe was also more cautious and attacked from 9,000-13,000 feet. But again waves of bombers came to target industrial sites and dropped 203 metric tonnes of high explosive bombs, 80 landmines attached to parachutes, and 800 firebomb canisters containing 96,000 incendiary bombs, so that the people called this the Fire-Blitz. Casualties were thankfully lower, with 150 killed and 157 seriously injured. Major damage, however, was inflicted on the Harbour Estate, the shipyards and the aircraft factories. The real suffering of the ordinary citizens of Belfast was immense, the horror unimaginable.

The story of the publication of this camera record of the Belfast Blitz of April and May 1941 is a tale in itself. First published immediately after the Blitz by the *Belfast Telegraph*, with most of the photographs by John Bonar Holmes, it has had a life of its own ever since. It was first brought to my attention by my friend David Adamson through his mother-in-law Sybil Ogilvie in 1984, and I published it under my own imprint, Pretani Press later that year. My mother and father Jane and John were in the North Down Air Raid Precautions (A.R.P.) and remembered the events well. Many refugees came to our village of Conlig because of the Blitz. 220,000 had left the city altogether. The kindness and consideration accorded to David and myself by Bob Crane, the Managing Director of the *Belfast Telegraph* and his archivist W. McAuley were exceptional, as was the support of Anna Crane, Bob's wife, who owned a landmark bookshop in Belfast.

There were also many others who helped: Violet Bowler, Chairman of Farset Youth and Community Development Ltd with its manager Jackie Hewitt; Ann Brown and Avril Lyons; Professor Ronnie Buchanan of the Institute of Irish Studies, Queen's University, Belfast; Ken Sterrett; Belfast Central Library; the Linen Hall Library; the Ulster Museum; the Ulster Folk and Transport Museum; the Ulster Society for Oral History; not forgetting Anne Johnston for the cartography and Jim Egner for the original cover illustrations; and last but not least Chris McGimpsey, whose father Harry taught me at Bangor Central Primary School, for the original introduction. I would also like to thank my wife Kerry for all her help and advice.

I had previously published in 1982 *The Identity of Ulster* and in 1983, *Colonel Paddy* by Patrick Marrinan and with the proceeds of both books was able to sponsor my young friend Edmund (Eddie) Irvine into motor racing. I was also able to publish for Lady Caroline Kinahan, the wife of Sir Robin, a former Lord Mayor of Belfast, her second book, *After the War Came ... Peace*. Sir Robin introduced me and my friend David Campbell, now Chairman of the Ulster Unionist Party, to Princess Alice, Duchess of Gloucester, who is recorded in the book visiting Belfast with her husband Henry just after the Blitz itself. Because of this connection we founded the Somme Association with the help of my friends Rev. Dr Ian Paisley, Eileen and Rhonda.

As our President, Princess Alice rededicated the Ulster Tower at Thiepval on 1st July, 1989. David Campbell and I had the privilege of visiting her regularly at Kensington Palace until she died on 29th October, 2004. But her son, Prince Richard, quondam Earl of Ulster, has continued in the role of President of the Somme Association, both in France and Gallipoli, and to him, and to the Royal Family as a whole, we will be eternally grateful. Our Association, with its most able Director, Carol Walker, has a permanent exhibition on the Blitz at the Somme Museum, Whitespots, Newtownards and there is a Home Front Exhibition at the

Northern Ireland War Memorial, Talbot Street, Belfast.

I am delighted that Colourpoint Books, who are the worthy successors of Pretani Press, have decided to republish this little but important book on the occasion of the 70th Anniversary of the Belfast Blitz, and once again we are indebted to the *Belfast Telegraph*. It remains essential that we never forget how the Ulster capital endured the most severe ordeal in its history, the heroism of our Civil Defence Services and the fortitude of our citizens. Nor those who lie unclaimed in the Millfield and City Cemeteries of Belfast. And most of all we must ensure, by maintaining peace in Europe, that this is a Belfast story which we must never allow to happen again.

Councillor Dr Ian Adamson OBE,
High Sheriff of Belfast

BELFAST RAID SEVERE AND SUSTAINED

Casualties Not So Heavy

"Heavy and sustained" is the official description of Sunday night's air raid on Belfast.

A joint communiqué issued by the Northern Ireland Ministry of Public Security and the R.A.F. Headquarters in Northern Ireland, at noon, stated:

"Large numbers of incendiary and high explosive bombs were dropped and there was much damage to commercial, industrial and residential property."

"The casualties will not be as heavy as at first feared," the statement adds, "and the loss of life as been less than was expected in view of the intensity of the attack."

POINTS FROM THE RAID

Portion of a flax spinning mill was cut away by a direct hit. One remarkable result of the raid was the "invasion" of recruiting offices and hundreds of men rushed to join the colours. In recruiting centres all over the Province Ulster thus answer to

DEATH AND DESTRUC

Buildings cleft in twain, clean cut as though with dwelling-houses reduced to a mere mass of rubl a grim picture of the savage "blitz".

One portion of Belfast bore traces of the terrific p received, and bed linen, curtains, etc., were flying fro across the road.

One area in particular was a real scene of destructi working-class houses were completely flattened to the When a "Telegraph" reporter visited the district he was a real scene of death and destr

Carry On, Belfast

(Belfast Telegraph 19th April, 1941)

The blitz has left very little of the windows of premises in one area, but "thumbs up" is the attitude of businessmen and householders alike. Some humorous phrases have been pasted up, but one businessman at all events is frank about it. On the only remaining pane of glass in his drapery establishment he has painted up the following:–

Business as usual.
I never liked window-dressing anyway.
Now I've got a good excuse for not doing it.
CARRY ON, BELFAST.

(Belfast Telegraph 16th April, 1941)

ULSTER BEARS THE FULL BRUNT OF NAZI VICIOUSNESS

The following joint communiqué issued by the Ministry of Public Security, Northern Ireland, and the Headquarters of the R.A.F., Northern Ireland:

"Belfast bore the brunt of the indiscriminate enemy air attacks carried out against Northern Ireland during the night.

Shortly after the alert had been sounded high explosive and incendiary bombs were dropped at random over the city.

A considerable number fell in residential and shopping areas, causing numerous casualties, many of which, it is feared, are fatal.

Other bombs caused damage to commercial and industrial premises.

Whilst the enemy were being met by a spirited defence from the A.A. guns, the various A.R.P., A.F.S., and other Civil Defence units were carrying out their duties with courage and devotion under conditions of difficulty and danger.

In other areas in Northern Ireland the intensity of the attack was not so severe, and the casualties were on a correspondingly smaller scale."

DIRECT HIT MADE ON SHELTER
Little Family Wiped Out

A number of people were wiped out when a street shelter in which they had taken refuge received a direct hit. A father, mother, and their little son were among those lost. An A.R.P.

the "Telegraph" that the detonation was terrific, and she thought the whole street of houses had been destroyed. Clouds of dust almost choked her. A mission hall in the same street was

City hospitals suffered grievously in the blitz, among them the Ulster Hospital for Women and Children on Templemore Avenue. These pictures of the front and rear of the hospital show the severe damage caused.

GAS CASUALTIES

A block of shops at Newcastle Street on the Newtownards Road, which came to grief.

Belongings and furniture being salvaged from homes in Westbourne Street, Newtownards Road.

Damage to Ballymacarrett library on Templemore Avenue.

Only the walls remain of Strand Public Elementary School.

Section of a gigantic bomb crater in Ravenscroft Avenue, Newtownards Road, where there were numerous casualties.

The tower of St Patrick's Church on the Newtownards Road overlooks the cleared land at Westbourne Street with the ruins of Ballymacarrett library (centre right) currently being dismantled.

Part of the damage to an oil tanker under construction.

A fascinating panoramic view of part of the Harland and Wolff shipyard, damaged by air raids, showing the complete destruction the area suffered. Note the barrage balloon tethered in the right of the picture.

Part of the twisted stern framing of a corvette at Harland and Wolff. Three vessels nearing completion suffered direct hits in the raids.

Destruction at the Harland and Wolff main office. With concerted targeting destroying all the major works, production in the shipyards virtually stopped.

Harland and Wolff power station grid for the main office, damaged by air raids.

Belfast Corporation Tramways, run by the City Council, carried on despite the blitz, but not without its losses. Bombs fell both inside and outside this depot in Salisbury Avenue on the Antrim Road.

The burnt shell of the LMS NCC railway station frontage on York Road. Only a small portion of the building, designed by renowned architect Sir Charles Lanyon, was retained in the rebuilding.

A breakdown gang works with a crane to dispose of debris in what remains of the Goods Shed.

A bird's eye view of the LMS NCC passenger platforms at the York Road terminus, taken from the adjacent Midland Hotel on Whitla Street, which was also destroyed.

The grand station lost the large overall semi-circular glass roofs which covered the passenger platforms at the concourse end. Sadly these were never replaced after the war.

Twisted steelwork litters the site after the raids. Note how the number plates for the destroyed wagons have been repositioned for the photograph.

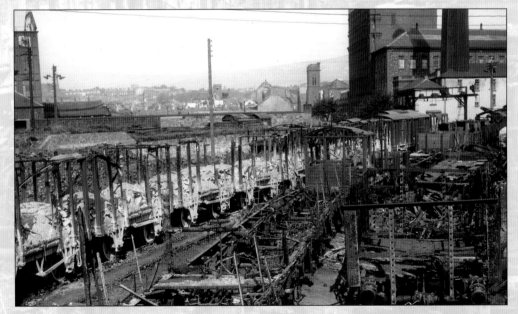

The scale of the LMS Railway's losses can be seen in this image of wrecked goods trains in a the marshalling yard. Although 21 carriages and dozens of wagons were lost, miraculously no locomotives were destroyed. In the coming months they were stabled at Greenisland during the night as a precaution.

Firemen deal with the aftermath of the raid while local residents inspect the damage to the exterior of the York Road station.

A work gang continues to clear up the damage. A sign amongst the piles of bricks warns "Caution Bomb Crater".

24

The Banqueting Hall in the Belfast City Hall, bore the brunt of the damage after an explosion.

The Hall was the scene of many historic functions, pictured here before bomb damage.

BOMBS ON BELFAST – THE BLITZ 1941

An exterior view of Belfast City Hall showing the damaged roof above the Banqueting Hall.

Workmen clearing the debris from the roof.

St. Anne's Cathedral had a very narrow escape from the bombs, when most of Donegall Street was reduced to rubble.

The same area after clearance, showing a new side view of the Cathedral from the corner of Royal Avenue. The site now holds the Belfast Campus of the University of Ulster.

Another view of the devastation beside St Anne's Cathedral, viewed from York Street.

And again after clearance – note the single shop still open for business (minus two floors!)

Demolishing Hazlett's store in North Street.

looking from North Street towards the 'Northern Whig' office in Bridge Street.

Many fine old buildings in central Belfast were lost in the raids, as here at the corner of Rosemary Street and North Street.

Billowing flames envelop the same corner during the raid.

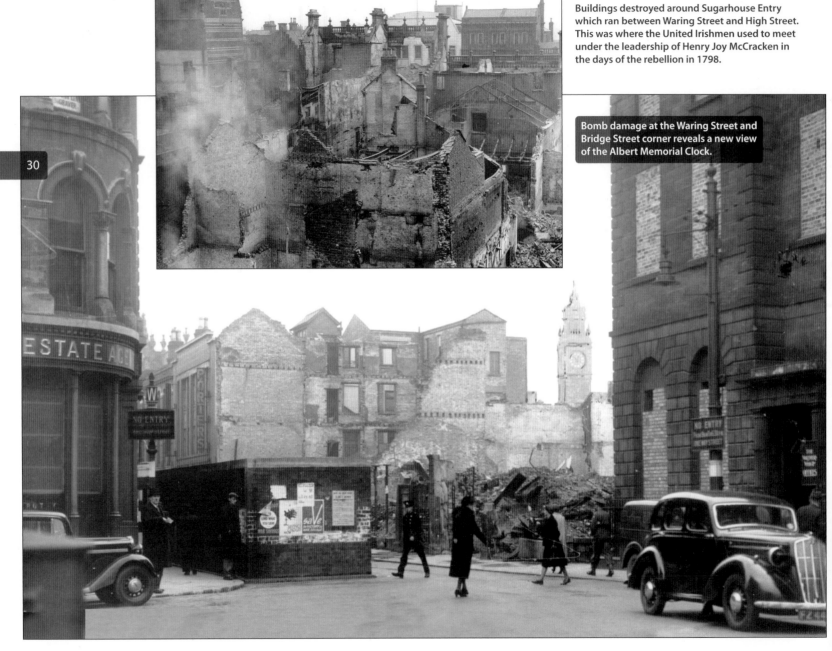

Buildings destroyed around Sugarhouse Entry which ran between Waring Street and High Street. This was where the United Irishmen used to meet under the leadership of Henry Joy McCracken in the days of the rebellion in 1798.

Bomb damage at the Waring Street and Bridge Street corner reveals a new view of the Albert Memorial Clock.

A steamroller being used to pull down buildings in Waring Street.

The corner of Waring Street and Victoria Street as seen from the Albert Memorial Clock. St Anne's Cathedral can be seen in the top left of the picture.

A large building gutted on the corner of Tomb Street and Albert Square, opposite the Custom House.

A panorama of the Victoria Street and High Street corner viewed from in front of the Albert Memorial Clock. The site is now occupied by the distinctive Transport House, built in 1959, and, remarkably, the building to the left of centre still stands.

A view of High Street looking towards Royal Avenue before the bombs fell.

The same area of High Street after the blitz. Taken from the Albert Memorial Clock, this view gives a clear impression of the devastation in the City Centre.

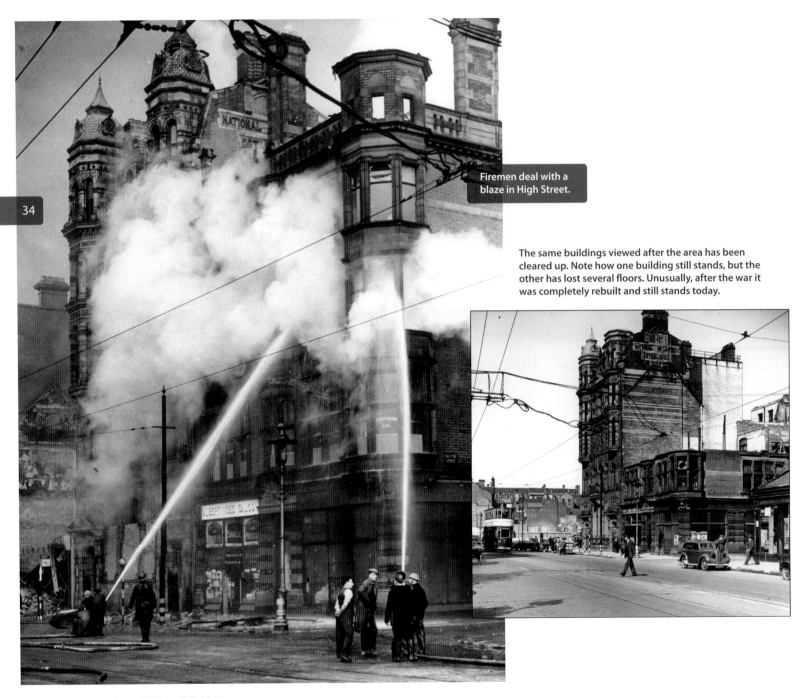

Firemen deal with a blaze in High Street.

The same buildings viewed after the area has been cleared up. Note how one building still stands, but the other has lost several floors. Unusually, after the war it was completely rebuilt and still stands today.

BOMBS ON BELFAST – THE BLITZ 1941

Smoke still rises from some rubble on High Street.

A steam shovel works hard clearing debris in High Street.

A view of High Street after being blitzed.

The same area of High Street as normal life resumes beside the shells of ruined buildings. The tram in the centre left is emerging from Bridge Street.

BOMBS ON BELFAST – THE BLITZ 1941

A photograph showing the typical aftermath of a raid. Bridge Street seen from High Street.

Two soldiers walk through the same area after the street has been cleared. The building in the centre rear of the image is the old Northern Whig office.

Bridge Street, one of the city's oldest and busiest streets, still served its purpose as a thoroughfare as men work to remove dangerous structures.

A chimney falling as more buildings are demolished on Bridge Street.

A soldier stands guard in this view of Bridge Street from North Street. The offices of *The Northern Whig and Belfast Post* stand scarred in the left of the picture.

Another view of Bridge Street toward High Street, taken from the roof of the Belfast Bank.

Firemen tackle a blaze in Castle Street where several blocks were gutted.

The vast open space created in the City Centre across Bridge Street and High Street after the blitz. Bridge Street was subsequently widened into the street we have today.

Three steamrollers converge to help demolish buildings on Castle Street.

A fireman hosing a building on Castle Lane, his ladder silhouetted against a flame-lit sky.

Quelling the flames on Victoria Street at the Anne Street corner. Note the badly damaged tramway cables brought down by the blast.

A panorama of the same Victoria Street and Anne Street corner after the clear up has been completed.

The Police Court, Chichester Street, in front of which a bomb exploded.

A water main laid between the tram tracks on Chichester Street to aid the fire defences by the ARP (Air Raid Precautions) and AFS (Auxiliary Fire Service) wardens.

Clearance work in progress at East Bridge Street.

Gloucester Street appears to be partially buried. The distinctive building in the background is Telephone House on Cromac Street.

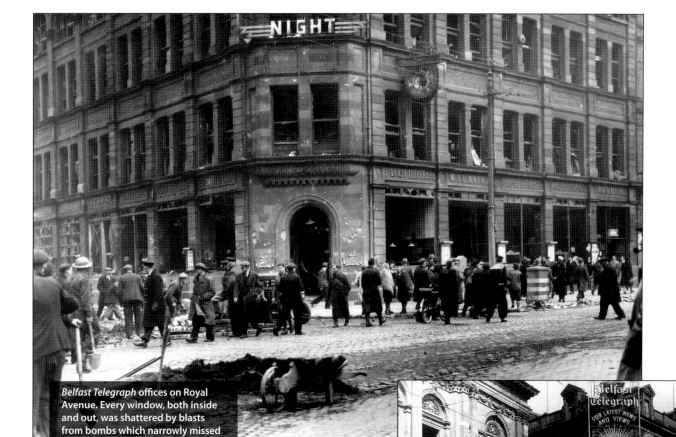

Belfast Telegraph offices on Royal Avenue. Every window, both inside and out, was shattered by blasts from bombs which narrowly missed the building.

The *Belfast Telegraph* offices boarded up but still going strong. The three Belfast morning papers were all published here for a period after the raid. The Belfast Central Library stands in the left of the picture.

The editorial offices inside the *Belfast Telegraph* continued in use despite the obvious damage.

Arthur Street in the distance, as seen from Donegall Place. The gap has been created by the destruction of Messrs. Brand's (Ulster Arcade) Emporium. The site is midway along the east side of Donegall Place and the building in the left of the photograph still stands.

The burnt out shell of Cavendish furniture store on Callender Street, with signs of clearance underway.

Workmen refitting glass on Robinson & Clever's landmark store on the corner of Donegall Place, and Donegal Square North.

48

The same mill frontage on York Street, each floor bearing its compliment of machinery, now reduced to scrap.

The impressive York Street Flax Spinning Co. Ltd, which was the largest of its kind in the world before the blitz.

The site after clearance, the great mill chimney being all that was left of the massive spinning works. Gallaher's famous tobacco factory is seen in the background of the photograph.

The rear of the flax mill in North Queen Street, where Grove Street and Vere Street intersect. Mounds of rubble mark where rows of workers dwellings once stood. Many were killed when most of the wall on one side of the mill collapsed on top of the small houses.

The view from Henry Street with smoke still rising from portions of the mill premises.

The International Bar on the corner of Donegall Street and York Street, still smoulders.

The facade of the International Bar attracting many glances before being pulled down.

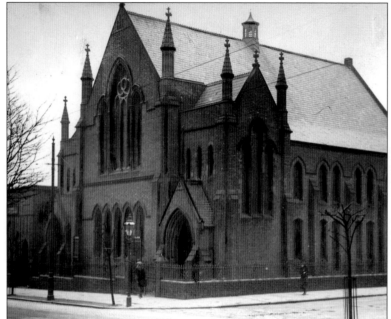

Macrory Memorial Presbyterian Church, Duncairn Gardens before the blitz.

The heavily damaged building in the aftermath.

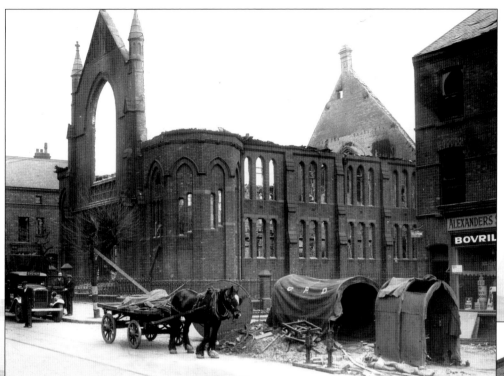

Duncairn Methodist Church after a bomb explosion.

St. Silas's Parish Church on the Oldpark Road.

Castleton Presbyterian Church, York Road.

Newington Presbyterian Church, Limestone Road.

Holy Trinity Church (off Clifton Street) minus its spire.

Crumlin Road Presbyterian Church outlined in fire.

The interior of St James's before the blitz.

St. James's Parish Church on the Antrim Road after the bomb raids.

York Street
Presbyterian
Church.

York Street Non-Subscribing
Presbyterian Church.

Men inspect the extensive damage to Newtownards Road Methodist Church.

A bomb crater at St. Matthew's Catholic Church on the Newtownards Road.

Clifton Street
Presbyterian Church,
both before and after it
suffered a direct hit in
the raid.

A view through the facade of Rosemary Street Presbyterian Church.

The completely destroyed interior – the church was never rebuilt.

A partially cleared area in Ballycarry and Ballynure Streets off the Oldpark Road.

Percy Street, in the Shankill area where 60 people were killed when an air raid shelter was hit.

The extensive damage on Eglinton Street just south of Carlisle Circus.

A work party clearing great heaps of rubble from Eglinton Street.

A view of Carlisle Circus Methodist Church across Eglinton Street and Carlisle Street.

The scene near Carlisle Circus after a bomb was dropped.

With a lack of available mechanical aid, these men are manually demolishing houses on the Antrim Road.

A gable falls as homes are demolished on the Antrim Road.

Soldiers undertaking a grim search amongst devastated buildings on the Antrim Road.

Burke Street at its junction with Annadale Street.

The morning after a raid in Annadale Street, where every house was destroyed.

Homeless people return to search in the ruins of Annadale Street (now Sheridan Street).

Ruins still smoulder – Annadale Street.

The Annadale Street area after clearance.

A bomb crater on Cliftonville Road. The blast destroyed a number of premises in the vicinity.

Heavy bombs fell at the junction of the Antrim Road and Duncairn Gardens, demolishing a number of houses.

Wrecked houses and businesses between Duncairn Gardens and Hillman Street.

The same area after clear up has been completed. Many parts of Belfast witnessed the creation of vast new areas of waste ground as a result of the blitz.

Wrecked homes and a wrecked car in Hughenden Avenue, Cavehill Road, illustrating perfectly how selective the bomb damage could be between houses.

Graphic damage to some more modern houses in Sunningdale Park, Cavehill Road, by a large parachute mine.

Blitz-scarred Shandarragh Park, also on the Cavehill Road.

Salvage work begins in Sunningdale Park, Cavehill Road.

A bomb site with demolished shelter in Atlantic Avenue, Antrim Road, illustrating that even reinforced concrete was sometimes inadequate protection.

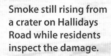

Smoke still rising from a crater on Hallidays Road while residents inspect the damage.

A now vacant space on York Road with Castleton Presbyterian Church (now Alexandra Presbyterian) in the background.

Damaged property on York Road with many curious children.

Gutted remains in York Park off the Shore Road.

The bombed area at York Crescent off the Shore Road.

Whitewell Road damaged after bombings.

Beds and baths exposed by the bombs, Whitewell Road. For many thousands the loss of their homes was complete.

76

Residents of Ballyclare Street, Oldpark Road, salvaging what they can from the ruins.

Three more residents carefully load a vehicle on the York Road.

Workmen spreading out rubble from destroyed buildings on waste ground.

Standing amid the remains of an air raid shelter in Thorndyke Street, Albertbridge Road. In the background are houses wrecked by the blast.

Several Military Police taking refreshments.

Ballymoney mobile canteen serving some soldiers with tea and sandwiches.

Some Auxiliary firemen fighting the flames in York Street.

Soldiers, seen here working hard in York Street, performed much of the clear up service throughout the city.

Amidst the rubble some soldiers rest with a salvaged gramophone.

Putting a brave face on things, while taking refreshments.

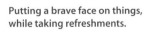

More work to be done! Clearing debris in Walton Street, Crumlin Road.

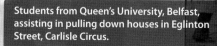

Students from Queen's University, Belfast, assisting in pulling down houses in Eglinton Street, Carlisle Circus.

AFS who rendered invaluable aid in fighting out-breaks of fire and in rescue work, being inspected by Rt Honourable J.C. MacDermott, K.C. (then Minister of Public Security).

HRH Duke of Gloucester inspecting air raid damage in Percy Street, Shankill.

A stretcher party passing Crumlin Road Presbyterian Church on an errand of mercy, while the flames devour the building.

Salvaging furniture at Southport Street and Manor Street corner, Oldpark Road.

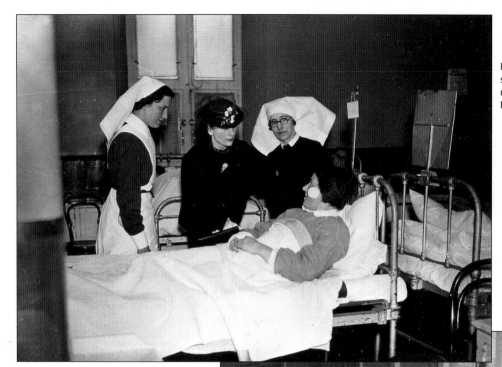

Duchess of Gloucester speaking to an air raid victim at Union Hospital.

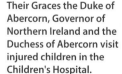

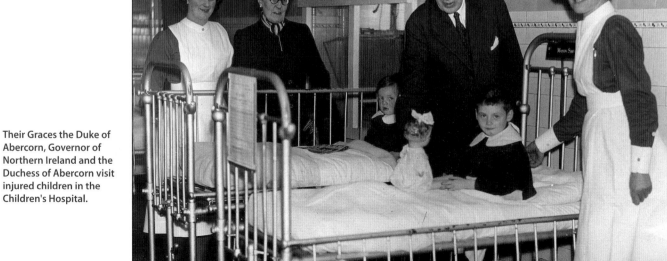

Their Graces the Duke of Abercorn, Governor of Northern Ireland and the Duchess of Abercorn visit injured children in the Children's Hospital.

Londonderry mobile canteen, with a group of soldiers, taking a break from demolition.

Musical interlude. An impromptu organ recital on York Street.

A working party at Oldpark Presbyterian Church, takes a break to pose amongst the debris.

A rather mischievous looking group of children being evacuated at the railway station!

A trio of nervous evacuees on their way to safety – or should that be a quartet?

Children being evacuated at the railway station after the April blitz.

Historical Picture Postcards

This and 6,000 more historical images for you to view and buy at
www.belfasttelegraph.co.uk/postcards